BAD A$$
CEO

HOW TO PROTECT YOUR SELF INTEREST, PURSUE REAL POWER AND WEALTH AND SHAPE YOURSELF TO BE ECONOMICALLY COMPETITIVE

Ray Bolden

ISBN-13: 978-0692705285 (Bold Ambition Worldwide, LLC)
ISBN-10: 0692705287

Dedication

If you don't understand freedom and power, what it is and how it works, everything else that you've been taught will confuse you. This is dedicated to the millions of men and women around the world who are struggling unsuccessfully to see beyond what's right in front of them.

Author's Note

Everybody wants to live under their own rules and do what they want to do when they want to do it. This book is giving you that chance, right here; right now…what are you going to do?

Table of Contents

Preface

Why is it that you don't know what to do to create a viable means to empower yourself? Is it that you lack the resources to solve your problems or is it that you lack the incentive and commitment? On one level, this could be a rhetorical question. We look for approval, guidance and support. We reason that since we don't have the finances and the power that we want, we need to be saved by something or somebody else. The critical question you need to ask yourself is: "What's your definition of freedom?" This was the major catalyst for my previous books *BAD BOYS FINI$H RICH* and *REBELLIOU$ WEALTH.*

So where do we place the blame? A deeper issue is how much blame do we place on ourselves? What do you think? We give those who we perceive to be more successful too much credit. You should not be sitting idly by, watching as other people progress, move up and move ahead. You have just as much right to prosperity as others who you view as being more successful and a better chance of achieving it through your own initiative. We have the right to be healthy, happy and fully engaged citizens without living under the shadow of perceived economic inferiority. After years and years of frustration, I finally realized that I was not going to win until I stopped thinking and acting as though the only way to empower myself and be self-reliant was to do it from society's point of view. Questioning authority is your prerogative and a part of being self-reliant. It was at this point that I decided to do my own research. What I found deeply disturbed me, but there was a card I had yet to play…being a *BAD A$$ CEO,* so I was emboldened by a rather extraordinary, even revolutionary idea. I built an empire on a foundation of attitude/ being bad / being rebellious / being a bad boy / and not being a team player and for the first time, I was reading something that sounded like me, that looked like me and felt like me. I believe that once you change the vision of yourself, you will blaze a new path of unlimited possibilities. I stopped feeling sorry for myself and I stopped feeling economically inferior. It's hard to imagine where I'd be today if not for my attitude. I share this story not to boast, but to speak of my success and the power of being a *BAD A$$ CEO*. With *BAD A$$ CEO,* all things are possible. There is no better time than now to shift your mind. No better time to use your resources and talents to soar. This book is provocative and powerful. It insulates all aspects of our lives, yet for some it is not an acceptable topic of discussion. That is not the reality. It's time for a serious dialogue and a change in strategies. The purpose of this book is to illuminate and examine the strategies and techniques that can be used to practice economic empowerment in a capitalistic democracy by creating your own information business.

For many of us, life is and has always been, considered fragile and unpredictable so some readers might think that this book is too optimistic because it breaks new ground by offering a hard and honest look at how to best resolve and finally terminate accepting a subordinate position. The purpose is not to criticize but to analyze and propose a reasonable solution. Since tomorrow is never promised, we must be the creators of our own destinies and you have a very powerful option. *BAD A$$ CEO* is a sleeping giant that if properly mobilized could achieve economic power. It reinforces your uniqueness and right to develop an independent system that addresses your distinct needs and desires. These pages will outline multi-tiered, action-oriented strategies but without complete buy-in and radical action it's power is useless. I am asking you to put your mind where your future can be. In other words, this is not just a book; it's a mission…One that you can accomplish. *BAD A$$ CEO* is designed to not only show you what's right, but to make it sexy, give it swag and all the other things most people want to be. Each of us wants our own turf, our own rules, our own way of doing things and especially our own opinion. It's quite nice to be considered an exception to the norm. Once you commit yourself to seeing yourself as a *BAD A$$ CEO* and once you shift your loyalty and place being a *BAD A$$*

CEO in proper perspective, the master puppeteer will no longer pull your strings.

Bad Ass

Function:

Noun

1. Unquestionable authority.
2. An ultra-cool motherfucker.
3. Radiates confidence in everything he/she does and fears nobody.
4. Someone who totally owns who he/she is.
5. No obligation whatsoever to justify his/her beliefs, values, convictions, morals etc. with anyone.
6. Complete freedom.

.

BAD A$$ CEO!

"In America I am the part you won't recognize, but get used to me. Black, confident, cocky; my name not yours; my religion, not yours; my goals, my own; get used to me!"

~ Muhammed Ali

Introduction

THE RISE OF THE BAD A$$ MESSIAH

Power plays a critical role in America. Though you can't see it, taste it or touch it, you sense its presence and attest to its strength and potency. According to Webster's Dictionary, power is defined as the ability to bring about fulfillment of one's desires and needs. And according to Economist Thomas Sowell, power is not simply the ability to get something done, but to get it done despite the resistance and opposition of others. This is the definition that I refer to in this book. The most common way people give up their power is by thinking that they don't have any, so to quote the character Eli Gold from the TV show The Good Wife, "This is like everything else, it's about power and we are making it easy for them." Power determines the quality of your life and *BAD A$$ CEO* allows you to possess and exercise control over your own power rather than seeking access to another's power. And the final decision to use any particular form of control belongs to the power-holder, aka *BAD A$$ CEO.*

Self-empowerment is a true path to self-reliance and economic empowerment, but it requires a plan of action. I am engaged in the field of systematic persuasion and my goal is for you to fully understand the *BAD A$$ CEO* phenomenon. It's yours to define for yourself what it means to be a *BAD A$$ CEO.* All that's needed is a new way of thinking and acting. There are many excuses for not accepting the *BAD A$$ CEO* way of life, but if you are reading these words, you are obviously ready to take the necessary action to empower yourself in every possible way. Now I need to clarify that simply having power doesn't guarantee wealth. To succeed you must see yourself as distinct and powerful. You must organize to direct your own future and long-term best interest and *BAD A$$ CEO* is an effective strategy for getting vitally needed resources. *BAD A$$ CEO* isn't geared to change your mind. It's a mission to create a new mindset. It is positive artistry without resorting to exploitive, negative or denigrating tactics. It truly brings to light that you may not have all the power you want, but you have all the power you need to empower yourself. Why? Because somewhere in your journey, you have turned over control of your life and destiny. You've been conditioned to turn your personal power over to men and women who encourage you to wait on external forces. Now, your silence must be broken, inaction must be reversed and your self-worth must be reinforced. WARNING: Unless you are thoroughly fed up with your situation, *BAD A$$ CEO* will not help. You now have in your possession the guide to a new way of thinking: a way of thinking that stresses the idea that you can own and control your own life. Of all the disciplines and forces none is more powerful than *BAD A$$ CEO*.

Personally, I was restless for a basic kind of power and freedom that was crazy at best and arrogant at worst. I had no time for formalities or the seeking of advice or reassurance, I had to move forward. There was no point in discussing it. All I knew is that I had to go because the greatest movements in history began with a change of consciousness and make no mistake about it, *BAD A$$ CEO* is a very effective tool for creating new consciousness. You are joining and implementing the most aggressive campaign of like-minded individuals that you've ever engaged in. God is saying, "I've given you power; "Get up! It's time to go!" Maintaining the status quo has allowed you to make choices, but until now, you have limited your enjoyment of life. It is time to leave that in the past. The attitude of being a *BAD A$$ CEO* gives you a chance to truly live. It's as simple as that. The message is clear, consistent, ubiquitous and loud as well as positive, realistic and compelling so there's no reasonable excuse for inaction. So in order to get the most out of this book, it's imperative that you follow a few simple guidelines in order to receive its full benefits.

1. Aspire to greatness, even if you do not achieve fame, success, and money! As you read each chapter, take a minute to change your state of mind. Pretend that you are already a *BAD A$$ CEO* and do each lesson as if there is no possibility of failure.

2. Play by a new set of rules…"Yours!" Really let the truth of these ideas sink in. Even if you can't truly believe it yet, pretend that you truly believe it with all your heart and soul.

3. Free yourself from who society tells you that you are supposed to be! Feel the truth of the words by reading the words, sentences, paragraphs and quotes that stand out to you over and over again.

4. Push the envelope and boldly brandish your ambition! Take definite immediate action on what you learn and sell yourself and build the worth of your stock!

Economic power has always been the greatest source of power for individuals in America. Being a *BAD A$$ CEO* is a prerequisite. Our habits, customs and motivators are influenced by hope and symbolism. *BAD A$$ CEO* is about you giving yourself the freedom to be individuals and to be unique. The major problem is that we don't see ourselves as *BAD A$$ CEOs*. The most vital lessons you will learn from this book are how to approach life with a *BAD A$$ CEO* attitude and the skills to handle whatever challenges come your way with confidence and ease. This is what *BAD A$$ CEO* is all about. You'll discover the keys to a successful *BAD A$$ CEO* mindset and how to change the negative beliefs that hold you back from living the life you desire. Have you ever wanted something that's beyond your reach? An experience like nothing you could ever possess in real life? Now imagine a place where there are no laws, no rules or consequences. The only limits are those of your own imagination. Welcome to *BAD A$$ CEO*. A world of endless possibilities where you can have and do anything you want.

STEP ONE

Lead...Never, ever, ever follow

BAD A$$ CEO!

"You are scared of me because you can't control me. You don't and you never will. But that doesn't mean I am your enemy!"

~ Superman

Chapter One

THE MOST POWERFUL POSITION IN THE WORLD

(Aspire to greatness, even if you do not
achieve fame, success, and money!)

In a Capitalistic society, many of us have allowed ourselves to be reduced to a dollar bill. For many, an internalized sense of limitation has been embedded into our psyches. It's been ingrained in us from a very young age, "get out there. Work hard every day. Do the best you can. And you'll grow in your career and do well in life." That's been ingrained in us by our parents, and by society, from day one. What they don't teach us are the unwritten rules of the game. Many don't even know how the game is really played. Hell, some don't even call it a game. So we come into this work world thinking that if we bust our ass and put in twelve-hour days and work on the weekends, and neglect our families and we work very, very, very, very, very, very hard, then we will achieve high levels of success in life. Now having said that, there is an element of truth to that, but it is indeed relegated to a small minority. In most cases, when you get to certain levels within an organization, it takes a lot more than just performance to excel to the next level.

So what happened? How did mediocrity overpower internal certainty? What powerful force caused many of us to revert to the slave master's dictate and accept a subordinate position? If you understand that you as an individual represent wealth, then you realize that you have human capital. According to Maslow, greatness can only be achieved by Self-Actualization. When you are self-actualized, you become unstoppable even if you do not have money, a good job, a great education, professional credentials, good health or a roof over your head. This means we don't all have to play by the same rules and have the same game plan. I know of a way to win, to get success and its spoils and get away with it without losing your soul. So I'm rewriting the old script. I'm advocating a system designed for freethinkers and creating financially literate people who can prosper in a capitalist system. If you want to feel more secure about your future, you need to play by a new set of rules and this book will teach you those rules and how to use them to your advantage.

THE REALITY OF GREATNESS

The word Bad Ass functions as a noun and can be defined as an ultra-cool motherfucker who totally owns who he/she is, radiates confidence in everything he/she does and fears nobody because they have no obligation whatsoever to justify their beliefs, values, convictions, morals etc. with anyone because they have unquestionable authority and complete freedom. Webster's dictionary defines a CEO as: the highest-ranking person in a company or other institution, charged with maximizing the value of the entity, responsible for making managerial decisions and ultimately dealing with the higher-level strategy of the company and directing its overall growth. As I told you in my previous book *REBELLIOU$ WEALTH*, these two definitions mean that taking 100% responsibility for your life means you acknowledge that you create everything that happens to you and that you are the cause of all you experience. Today high school kids and college dropouts are billionaires and it's because they are entrepreneurs, not employees... aka *BAD A$$ CEOs*. The reason for this is that they deliberately and thoughtfully recognize that being a *BAD A$$ CEO* comes from the inside out and the way you control your own destiny and economic empowerment is by building your own personal brand and by building it authentically. Instead of trying to change the system, they are working to create their own system. It's a waste of time to criticize and complain about a system that will never change. Instead of complaining, you should ask, how can I become a *BAD A$$ CEO? BAD A$$ CEO* is based on the premise that you are the founder, president and 100 percent stockholder in your own company, both personally and professionally. In other words,

BAD A$$ CEO is a whole new way of thinking about yourself and how you relate to the world around you and this book is designed to heighten your awareness and expand your personal paradigm so that you can discover the *BAD A$$ CEO* within. This is how the famous writer Mark Twain describes it, "Inherently, each of us has the substance within to achieve whatever our goals and dreams define. What is missing from each of us is the training, education, knowledge and insight to use what we already have."

Old behavior models and learned helplessness stand between you and your chosen path. Most of this is not real, it's imagined, yet you treat them like they are the "Big Boss" that you have to get permission from before you can achieve your dreams. The value of the end game needs to be what matters to you. You're labeled in hundreds of ways by thousands of people, but how much of it have you consciously controlled? How much have you consciously created? How much of what's known about you is authentic to you, and how much is merely the perception of others? A Bad Ass is often thought of negatively, but being a *BAD A$$ CEO* can be a powerful tool. But it doesn't come easy. It takes real effort, imagination and follow through. This requires a fundamental change in your assumptions. You must move from the mind-set of "I am a subordinate" to "I am a *BAD A$$ CEO*." In essence, you have to unlearn what you have learned. By doing so, you take control of your destiny and hold the key to playing your own game within the game according to its new rules. *BAD A$$ CEO* is not about being smarter than everyone else, or being the person with all the right answers and it doesn't care about your age, your job experience, your race or your gender. It also doesn't care about your college degree. *BAD A$$ CEO* is a measure that's driven internally. The solution isn't to change the system but to play your own game within the game.

AN ENTIRE ECONOMY
THAT YOU CANNOT SEE

Many of you have accepted society's version of you and decided that society's version was the best that you could be. The point of this book is to open your eyes to the power you have to control your self-reliance and economic empowerment. The only way to win is to admit that you are on your own, learn to make your own decisions and trust your own judgement. That or continue to be a pawn in someone else's game. Through my company *BOLD Ambition Worldwide*, I've found a way to win. Bold Ambition was founded to provide educational products and mentorship programs for people not accustomed to having complete control of their lives so that they can become self-reliant and create economic empowerment for themselves. The challenge for me was attempting to define myself. It's common for people to struggle to define themselves. Everyone asks themselves certain general questions: What are my values? What principles do I stand for? Having specific answers to these questions is of paramount importance. I know you want to live like you want to live and there really is such a thing as a win-win situation! I never needed anyone's approval because from the start, I came into the game as a *BAD A$$ CEO*. That gave me the freedom to be myself which is the secret to any long term success. Personally, I decided to study the game of self-reliance and play the game with an attitude according to my own rules. I was prepared to think differently and more creatively. I had a dream about how I could be successful in my own way so I did what I had to do to make my dream of personal success come true. I took what I learned and applied that knowledge to my own game within the game. Before I started, I chose to become a *BAD A$$ CEO* which meant that I would take total control of my life and hold myself 100% accountable for my own success. Today I'm reaping the benefits of that choice. Once I made that choice, I had no time for formalities or the seeking of advice or reassurance, I had to move forward. There was no point in discussing it. All I knew is that I had to go. Old-school thinking says go to school, get good grades, graduate, get a good job, save 10%, invest in the stock market, max out your 401K, slash your

28

credit cards, and clip coupons then someday, when you are about 65 years old, you will be rich. Remember, the subtitle of this book is "How to protect your self-interest, pursue real power and wealth and shape yourself to be economically competitive", not how to graduate from college, wait for someone to hopefully give you a job then be a subordinate. The premise behind old school thinking is that economic success is confined to people who go to school, get good jobs and get big titles behind their names. Here we completely explode that notion. Society has conditioned us to believe that this is the perfect plan and the problem is we've been brainwashed to accept it. The brainwashing is amazing, deep and deliberate in our society. College education in the United States is increasingly unaffordable and the average college graduate leaves school more than $25,000 in debt. Today in the United States there is a massive amount of economic anxiety. Unemployment is much too high, wages and income are too low, millions of Americans are struggling to find affordable health care and the gap between the very rich and everyone else is growing wider. When you take a step back and seriously take a look at it, it means that we are lending money to people who can't pay it back to train them for jobs that no longer exist. Deep in our souls we know this, yet we continue to faithfully pledge obedience to this road map that is only a partial plan. Partial because according to this plan, your plan doesn't begin until after college, but there is no leverage and control. Regardless of how you slice it, with this plan you are hoping someone hires you and in some form gives you some type of power which makes you feel good about yourself. But this isn't power at all because it lacks leverage and although you may have a title behind your name, you really don't have control because it can all be taken away by budget cuts or changes in the economy. As I taught you in *REBELLIOUS WEALTH*, "There is a big difference between being in charge and being in control." With this plan, you buy into the myth that college ensures a job and you become one of many cogs in a wheel with very limited leverage and limited control. The actors are different, but the stage is always the same and you become content living the expectant life preordained by society. As a result, we spend our lives marching, hoping, praying, working, begging, bowing, and compromising, with the expectation that we will be rewarded for our education and good behavior. Unfortunately, it can cause many of us to abandon the person we were meant to be, all for the sake of trying to become somebody else. If you require proof, look no further than the person that you see in the mirror.

GRAB YOUR NUTS AND
REFUSE TO BE IGNORED

Now don't get me wrong, I am a 100% advocate for higher education. The difference is I advocate leading rather than following. What this means is that with all forms of education, college or otherwise, you should always be asking yourself how can this information help me to protect my self-interest, pursue real power and wealth and shape myself to be economically competitive? Now that doesn't mean simply having a high paying job, a big house or a fancy car, because for most people those material items are all financed with debt. If you want to live unlike everyone else, you can't be like everyone else. It's your responsibility as a *BAD A$$ CEO* to transcend mediocrity. You need to reverse engineer and deconstruct this strategy. Ask yourself this: Which experience is more important? The experience of a menial job designed to pay your bills? Or the experience (and failures) of creating something that could provide you financial freedom for a lifetime without ever having to hold a job again? The American dream is: you either are the one that pursued your dream or you wake up and you work for the person that did. So I encourage you to get a good education, develop some on-the-job experience, and then use your education to start your own business. The end goal is to leave school being even more capable of being financially independent and financially secure.

If you want to live that life, you have to be a *BAD A$$ CEO*. As I told you in my previous books *BAD BOYS FINI$H RICH* and *REBELIOU$*

WEALTH, you have been seduced into believing that you don't have any real power. That you have to earn it or it has to be given to you. Instead of limiting our potential by thinking of ourselves in traditional, narrowly defined ways that we've been taught, we must expand the boundaries of our thinking so that we begin to think and act like a successful company. Think *BAD A$$ CEO*.

The cornerstone of *BAD A$$ CEO* is that the same principles that successful companies use to create their fair market value and generate millions of dollars in profits can be applied to the lives of average people. People like you and me to dramatically increase your value. Let's up the stakes a little bit. If you could make the world the way you wanted it to be, what would you do? If you could change anything, if you could do anything, what's the first thing you would do? No matter what, you have the freedom to make a choice even if no one seems to understand that. If you think my method is totally different from what you are doing, you are wrong. Let me explain. The amount of work that goes into your way of doing things and my way of doing things is the same, but the final result is different. Do not, regardless of your limited knowledge, subordinate yourself to anyone. The only defense is to control the playing field, and to do that, you have to be the boss. New-school thinking says that an average guy like me without any special skill or talent can make it big. Take heed to the words of TS Eliot, "Only those who will risk going too far can possibly find out how far one can go." If you are serious about attaining true success in this rapidly changing world, start with the premise that from both a financial and a personal point of view, your most valuable asset is not your job, your house, or your bank account. Plain and simple, it's your creative ability. Your creative mind has great value because it can solve problems. In other words, your *BAD A$$ CEO* attitude is your power, and you should never give your power away. The fact that so many people haven't discovered that they are BAD A$$ CEOs is the major reason why they simply toil away in mediocrity and follow the crowd. All things considered, your *BAD A$$ CEO* attitude is your greatest asset. To maximize the use of your *BAD A$$ CEO* attitude is to maximize the career and financial aspects of your life.

Recognize the latent genius within and stay in the habit of being a *BAD ASS CEO* if you want to attain true success in your life.

"BAD ASS CEO" – EXERCISE APPENDIX-A

Often, when we fail to get what we want we look for someone to blame. Sadly, this often leads us to point the finger at others, rather than accept that we are the source of the problem. Before you become a *BAD ASS CEO*, there are some very important questions that you need to ask yourself, so the following exercise is just one of several you will encounter within this course. These questions will better enable you to determine where you are in life along with, where you would like to be and what you need to do to get there. Coming up with good answers is far less important than taking the time to ask yourself tough questions, but be sure to answer truthfully. As simple as this may sound, many people are shocked by their answers. These questions are designed to ignite serious introspection, so ask yourself these questions regularly and you will make better, more effective decisions about your life and the actions you need to take.

- What's your definition of freedom? (Take some time with this & explain in detail)

- Can you achieve the freedom (financial or otherwise) that you want by following the masses?

- What do you want your legacy to be…Consumer or Producer?

- Are you willing to challenge traditional assumptions about education, life and work to discover new solutions that will allow you to shift the balance of power?

- What is your greatest asset?

- How can you use your asset to take control of your life and your circumstances?

STEP TWO

Build your own dream not someone else's

BAD A$$ CEO!

"This is the American Dream. I'm going to get all this shit!"

~ Russell Simmons

Chapter Two

A SCRIPT OF YOUR OWN DESIGN

(Never settle for less. If it's not what you
want; make it into what you want it to be)

In the twenty-first century, entrepreneurship is more than just an endeavor, it is an empowering mindset. Being entrepreneurial is an art rooted in the belief that there is always a way to use creativity, passion and inspired vision to create value in the world. This mindset leads people to create an entirely new school or religious institution that addresses an unmet need; transform a corporation to do new things in new ways or take something that already exists and make it better. Such thinking enables you to be more creative, more insightful and more innovative in your approach to both personal and professional matters. It fosters an ability to effectively navigate inevitable situations that force you to move beyond your comfort zone. Being a *BAD A$$ CEO* grounds you. It allows you to define yourself on your terms, as opposed to others defining you on their terms. It is simply not conforming to who society told you that you are supposed to be, but you creating your own path in life and in business. Coming to understand your particular personal brand unleashes a power within you that can transform your life and the lives of others so when society suggests that you should go in one direction, it's your *BAD A$$ CEO* attitude that gives you the self-confidence to know that you can choose to go down your own path. It answers the questions who am I? And what makes me unique? And with absolute blind determination and some necessary measure of faith and just plain grit it can answer the questions why do I exist? And where am I going? It simply requires your personal vision for the future and your commitment to what you need to learn to have the future you desire and deserve. *BAD A$$ CEO* is about having courage and taking action…even if you are afraid, and know you will make mistakes and possibly fail on your path to success and the life you want for yourself and your family. It's about picking yourself up when you fail and learning from your failures and mistakes. I didn't say it was fair. What I'm saying is that being a *BAD A$$ CEO* will assist you in seeing both sides of the story clearer. The key message here is that being a *BAD A$$ CEO* is about leveraging all of the resources at your disposal to create value in your world and use your talents to make a positive impact in your areas of influence. Is this starting to sound like too much of an unattainable fantasy to you? It shouldn't. If it is, you are likely too programmed with society's meaning of traditional success and need to experience a paradigm shift.

AN AVERAGE GUY WITHOUT ANY SPECIAL SKILL OR TALENT, WHO SOMEHOW MADE IT BIG

Today you have more flexibility to arrange your life just the way you want than at any other time in history. And if you don't design your own life plan, you'll fall into someone else's plan. I was never content with living the expectant life preordained by society. I can remember always thinking and imagining my life beyond where I was. I just had no clue how I was going to find it or where to start. I knew various ways to wealth but just couldn't execute them correctly. What was I doing wrong? What was holding me back? After all the years of research and books that I read, I was still no closer to wealth. The information I obtained wasn't feeding me. I wasn't fulfilled. My feeling from the books that I read was that they the authors are mainstream; I am not. I couldn't relate to the information that I read because I didn't feel that the information was created for people who think like me, act like me, dream like me, and have the same longings and aspirations. This tension I felt inside was more than just typical frustration. It also reflected unresolved issues related to my identity. I found it difficult to fully define myself. So what do I do? I'm still trying to figure out my life, trying to discover who I really am. If I was going to win, I needed to change. I decided to take control over something that many think is uncontrollable: My thinking! I made a decision about how I was going to live my life and during my pursuit of success, I discovered that it wasn't what I was doing but who I wanted to become that makes all the difference. I looked in the mirror and actually saw myself next to me, like a vision. I was looking down over myself. As I looked at myself, so much was running through my mind. It all starts with the person I am looking at, right here, right now! I thanked the man in the mirror for giving me permission to be great. I realized the purpose of the whole experience wasn't just about creating wealth and success; it was about deepening a relationship with myself. That experience changed my life. In an instant, I felt powerful. It was about taking control and knowing I had a choice. This lit a fire under me and incited me to seek out and become the best version of myself. I grew married to the idea of achieving the American Dream. I was a businessman. To make a long story short, I was a Capitalist. Knowing the difference in mindsets kept me going. My mind could see distinctions, subtle differences and things I had never seen before; I was crossing over to the other side. I was becoming a *BAD A$$ CEO*. Little did I know that roadblocks, detours and mistakes lay ahead, but my results would be indicative of my true self. I was in control of my life. Regardless of your field or industry, you can do the same.

Your job is to determine what is true for you. You need to create an authentic personal brand that transcends the gatekeepers, the critics, the haters who want to put a label on you. I did not let fear, frustration or doubt stop me from doing what I needed to do. I simply got to work building my businesses. I have the same fears as everybody else. However, I simply don't let fear stop me from doing what I have to do. Most people only see problems; I do my best to see the opportunities that the problem presents. Learning from my business mistakes was the best business school I could have ever attended and I am still in that school today. All those obstacles in your path are only obstacles because you're telling yourself they are. If you say you can't make it, you won't. If you say you can make it, you will. You are absolutely right about both. Even those who recognize the dead-end nature of their current position are often reluctant to change. Why? Reasons vary, but some are so caught up in the pursuit of status and material possessions that they neglect to find their true self. Take heed to the words of Dr. Thomas J. Stanley author of The Millionaire Next Door, "The pseudo-affluent are insecure about how they rank among the Joneses and the Smiths. Often their self-esteem rests on quicksand. In their minds, it is closely tied to how long they can continue to purchase the trappings of wealth. They strongly believe all economically successful people display their success through prestige products. The flip side of this has them believing that people who do not own prestige brands are not successful." It's always a shame to see a person's talents wasted. Success is not about flaunting your wealth. It's about a sense of accomplishment and the independence that comes with it. It's how we spend ourselves not our money that makes us rich. No matter how you spend your days, you have a clear choice. You can view your life in terms of responsibilities and obligations or you can view it as a contest, a challenge, an opportunity.

IN LIFE AND IN BUSINESS, IT'S ALWAYS PERSONAL; ALWAYS!

If you read *REBELLIOU$ WEALTH*, you may recall that the subtitle of the book was "How To Break The Rules (not the laws) To Create Your Own Economy. For many people, reading my book was a lifting of the veil, a disclosure of something hidden from the majority for the purpose of equipping you with the knowledge necessary to answer the question: "What can I do to create my own game within the game? Like its predecessor, the more corporately educated you are, the less sense the new rules of being a *BAD A$$ CEO* will make. Why? Because I was looked upon as just a nobody. What did I know about wanting to be somebody and what it took to thrive? I had to be the one to set the course of my life. As previously stated, I advocate a system designed for freethinkers and to create financially literate people who can prosper in a capitalist system so whether you agree or not, the fact remains that having a *BAD A$$ CEO* attitude is more important today than ever before. Your attitude is the story you tell the world. What do you want your narrative to be? I acted like I owned the whole fucking world. Which means you inhabit being a *BAD A$$ CEO* wholly and completely, adopting the mannerisms and attitude regardless of whether the cameras are rolling. Your goal is to uncover the best version of yourself. There's a direct correlation between how you perceive yourself and the level of confidence you project. I just decided that I was not going to be discouraged, not going to be a victim of my circumstances. I was going to manifest and make things happen and so I just didn't rest and I didn't doubt.

I have a well-earned reputation of being aggressive so when I walk into a room, you can feel my confidence radiating. It's because I'm using my BAD A$$ CEO attitude as motivation to be better. The essence of the *BAD A$$ CEO* rule is that having the correct information, mindset and attitude is much better than simply having money because: "A rich man may not need to fear being broke, for he knows the tactics that may be exorcised in order to regain his wealth." What I want you to do is to say I'm going to take my own journey and I'm going to totally shatter whatever limitations I have in my life. You kind of hope for these storybook endings in your life, but you don't always get them. But this time will be different because you will keep going to prove to yourself that you can do it and to give yourself the ability to see exactly what's possible. The reason this book is called *BAD A$$ CEO* is because it is about how to control your economy via your attitude, but my research has convinced me that there will always be those whose dreams are something that only happens in their sleep. Rather than become a *BAD A$$ CEO*, they just sit at home, watch TV and are angry and resentful of *BAD A$$ CEOs* who are more successful. For some it's essentially another world, but it makes no sense that one set of people can be in a cage but can't see the bars. Look, there is value in everybody, but this course serves to weed out the weak or the incapable. Becoming a *BAD ASS CEO* requires not only the desire for something better, but the willingness to act on that desire to achieve it. Thus the people who undertake such a journey are more likely to be the most motivated to make it. Everybody is always like, once I do this or do that, I'll be happy. It doesn't always work like that. *BAD ASS CEOs* are created when bold action is taken, when power is inserted in emphatic and creative ways and when your greatness reminds you that you are the baddest motherfucker in the room. The question is: Will you become a *BAD ASS CEO* and fortify your self-esteem, become self-reliant and empower yourself economically?

"BAD ASS CEO" – EXERCISE APPENDIX-B

The ultimate misery is living a life that is not your own. Therefore the choice must be made between the comforts of fitting in and pleasing others or your personal freedom to never settle for less and make your lifestyle into what you want it to be. It is absolutely essential that you think clearly about your mission of what it is that you want to do and the lifestyle that you want to live and that your values are embedded in it. So the following thought-provoking questions help you distinguish between new initiatives and demands that fit with your purpose, and those that don't. It's about you grabbing more power for yourself so asking yourself these questions often enough will keep you focused on your economic empowerment and willingness to improve your life in all areas.

- How clear are you about where you are going in life? (Do you know what you want? Do you know where you are going? Do you have plans to get to where you want to go?)

- How expressive are you about your life plans? (Can you express your thoughts and feelings to others when required or do you keep everything inside?)

- How competent are you in the things you do and want to do in life? (Do you do just enough to get by or do you need to learn more to become more competent?)

- How true to your beliefs and values do you live your life? (Do you live according to your beliefs and values or do you stray from them when things get a little tough? Do you listen to others first before putting your own values first?)

- How creative are you? (Do you express your creativity in life, at work, at home?)

- How confident are you? (Are you able to stand firm on your values and beliefs without caring what others think??)

- How open are you when it comes to trying new things? (Are you able to try new things without fear of failure or embarrassment?)

- How open are you to asking for help? (Can you ask for help, when needed, or do you quit when things get tough?)

- How much control do you have over your income and lifestyle? (If you had total freedom in life, what exactly would you do? If you could make your world the way you wanted it to be, what would you do? If you could change anything, what's the first thing you would do?

STEP THREE

Move billions of dollars around the world, and do it without having to take shit from anyone

BAD A$$ CEO!

"You were never created to live an average, get-by, short-end-of-the-stick life. You were created to be the head and not the tail, to lend and not borrow, to reign in life as a king. You have royalty in your blood; winning is in your DNA!"

~ Joel Osteen

Chapter Three

WEAR THE CROWN AND ADMIRE
THE WAY IT SPARKLES

(Make a bold power move)

W e all like to believe that there is one fabulous event or one big deal in life that is going to dramatically change our lives and many outside influences in society try to convince us that the good life is just around the corner. Unfortunately, you've been conditioned to accept normal based on society's definition of wealth. We have allowed our awareness of self-reliance to diminish and in doing so, we have caused our own suffering. We have forgotten that being free is a choice and that permission to move forward with boldness is never given by the fearful masses. We have patiently suffered long enough, hoping that one day someone will grant us more opportunity and happiness, but nothing external can save us.

So what does it take to succeed? Talent? Connections? Education? Wealth? Fortunately for most of us, it takes something very simple and accessible. Everything you need to understand about being a *BAD A$$ CEO* is in the mirror. You must not be afraid to look or be mystified. It's all there. This brings us back once again to the focus on economic empowerment and personal freedom. If you want to live unlike everyone else, you can't be like everyone else. You have to lead the pack and have everyone else follow you, so if taking action before the perfect conditions arise, or before we receive permission is unreasonable, then we must be unreasonable. We have the full power to exert our true strength, live our dreams and create wealth without fear or permission so let us not hope for mere chance to change our story; let us summon the courage to change it ourselves.

THE ULTIMATE SOURCE OF POWER

The exchange of some form of currency provides an economic and social foundation for almost everyone in the world and we find ourselves pulled in a variety of ways by a variety of social influences and cultural forces that sweep us into the slavery of debt. But we can't blame our financial slavery on anyone but ourselves. Too often we look at our financial situation and give in without a fight, as if we have no other choices, alternatives or resources than those dictated by outside influences. When we put our minds to it, set our actions in motion, and invest in ourselves, we can resist the power over us and create our own power. Everyone including myself always has room for growth and more financial discipline and accountability and one thing is certain there is no substitute for the vision of a *BAD A$$ CEO* forming a successful strategy and then implementing its execution and the best way to reinforce your *BAD A$$ CEO* attitude is to own and exercise the power you have to free yourself from financial slavery.

In order to get off to a good start you must reclaim power over your finances. The simplest way to do this is to list all of your debts in order from smallest balance to largest. List all of the debts you have except your home; even ones that you don't pay interest on. After listing the debts, pay the minimum payment on all the debts except the smallest. Use every dollar you can find from anywhere in your budget to pay the smallest debt until it is paid off. Once the smallest is paid off, use the payment from that debt, plus any extra money you can find to pay the next smallest debt. When debt number two is paid off, take the money that you used to pay on number one and number two and pay it, plus the extra money that you found on number three. When three is paid, move on to four and so on. Keep paying the minimums on all the debts except the smallest until it is paid off. Every time you pay one off, increase the amount that you pay on the next one down. All the money from your old debts and all the money you can find goes toward paying off the debt until it is gone. This process works. I have seen it work and once you see it work you will keep doing it because you will be excited about the fact that it works. As I write this book, today I am someone who is financially solvent…in economic terms "in the black." I paid off over $65,000 in debts in less than a year and became debt free except for my home, and I have a plan in place that will allow me to pay it off in 4 years. Now, I know where I am, where I am going and how I'm going to get there. Nothing else mattered, except getting out of debt. Financial pressure leads to desperation and desperation can make people quite vulnerable. Without freedom and a sense of power, I had no control over my life. It seemed like I couldn't win so this is for the person who needs what I needed when I first started trying to gain a clear understanding of financial matters, get control, get ahead and begin to implement a financial plan.

BAD A$$ CEO helps to relieve the pressures of financial oppression. It's a rescue program for the financially distressed and a comprehensive, motivational strategy to help people develop a new lifestyle. It was liberating to get the titles to my cars after paying them off in 10 months. Three years earlier than the life of the loans. It was a great accomplishment to pay off all of my credit cards. Not because I had some revelation that no one else has ever had; I was just trying to find a way for me and my family to thrive financially with the money I was already bringing home. I realized that to change my future, I had to change. I wanted to get completely out of debt so I could create real financial security. How you structure your blueprint for financial freedom is up to you and should be custom fit to your particular situation. If you incorporate this component into your strategy of life as a *BAD A$$ CEO*, you will have a key that unlocks your financial future.

IT ALWAYS SEEMS IMPOSSIBLE UNTIL IT'S DONE

There's only one real definition of financial independence and that is to be financially dependent on no one. And that's the goal of being a *BAD A$$ CEO*, to help you be completely independent of any job, any person…ever. Like Civil Rights leader Hosea Williams used to say, "Unbought and Unbossed!" Why am I wealthy versus the guy stuck in traffic driving to work in morning? I have freedom. I wake up and do what I want. I pursue my dreams. I write this book without worrying about how many will sell because I found an approach to life that revolutionized the way I looked at and used money. It opened me up to a secure future that I never thought that I would achieve. Why am I telling you this? Because you need to be the *BAD A$$ CEO* of your own life. Free to express who you truly are and to create and contribute to the world without paralyzing fear. I struggled, but learned to be free by taking baby steps. First, I scrimped and saved $1000 to use as my emergency fund. An emergency fund is money for those unexpected events in life you can't plan for such as my car breaking down or household appliances breaking like my kitchen faucet did. I know $1000 doesn't sound like a lot, but it helped me feel secure by creating a safety net of funds that could be used for emergency expenses while I used all of my other available cash to pay off my debts. Second, I made a list of all my debts from the smallest amount to largest amount that I owed. When I first made this list, it actually kind of hurt me because when I took a really good look at the numbers, I could clearly see how much money I was easily just giving away. After playing with the numbers I determined how much extra money could be applied towards the smallest debt and allocated as much of my monthly budget as I could toward debt elimination. I wanted to pay the absolute maximum amount that I could until the debt was gone.

Now I've heard this called the debt-snowball method, the debt stacking method or the Avalanche method, I used a variation of all three. Starting with the debt with the smallest balance, I paid as much as I could on that debt while I paid the minimum monthly balance on the other debts. Once the balance of first debt was paid off, it felt really good, and then I took the amount I was paying towards that debt plus the additional money that I was using to pay it off and applied it to the debt with the next lowest balance. Once the second debt was paid off, I repeated the process by adding the total I was paying to the minimum payment of the next debt, then the next debt and so on; continually combining the payments and knocking them out one by one until all of the debts were paid off. Third, to help keep our stress level down my wife and I sat down and calculated how much we would need to live on for six months and started saving to protect ourselves against life's unexpected events so that we would never be caught off guard. After living on the financial edge in the past, just hoping to get by, this safety net gave me confidence and was great for our financial well-being. For those of you who read *BAD BOYS FINI$H RICH*, you know I retired from the Air Force and also receive a pension so once the debt payments were gone and I had six-month's worth of living expenses in savings, my wife and I used the money that we were using to pay off the debt to build our financial future and long-term wealth by maximizing her companies 401(k) and our Roth IRAs along with creating and distributing our products and services for sale. Some of you are reading this and telling yourselves that it's inconceivable to even think about doing this. The key is you don't have to be an expert on financial management. The only thing worse than not having what you want, is not using what you have and obviously, desperate times call for desperate measures so use your *BAD A$$ CEO* attitude as if your life depends on it…because it does. How would you feel about yourself if you not only gained financial freedom, but actually accumulated wealth? By making a few adjustments and with laser-like focus and sustained dedication, you could be debt free in a much shorter period of time and save thousands of dollars in interest and fees.

The best educators teach from their own experiences and I practice what I preach. My primary motive in writing this book is for you to read, digest and discuss this material then present it to your children and family and friends before they become totally brainwashed by the consumer-driven society. If you were me, would you sit still and watch as your children and family and friends are forced to live a life of irrelevance and servitude?

Forced to live under a system that tells you what to say, what not to say, what to think, what not to think?

The issue of self-sufficiency and financial empowerment is sensitive and I live life on my terms. I got the guts to do it and I don't care what anybody thinks. It doesn't bother me one bit. My motivation is strictly this: I cannot let you win if you are trying to stop me from what I am trying to do. I succumb to wanting others to view me as successful just as much as the next person, but being a *BAD A$$ CEO* doesn't come from the outside, it comes from the inside, knowing who God created you to be. We must find peace within and become more self-reliant in creating the life we deserve. I'm brave enough to admit it and my main reason for confessing my weakness is to illustrate the magnitude of my desire to help people with their financial aptitude because so many people are afraid to demand more. I've heard it said that we are lions and lionesses living as mice; living small and distracted lives. Rather than chase our dreams with abandon, we sit around blaming and complaining. We must see the potential that we are leaving unrealized so that we might see a shining new path. I see a vision for a new way of life that can set so many people free to really live for the first time in their lives. If you didn't have to go to work and you didn't have to be concerned about having adequate financial security, then how would you spend your time? You can be rich at any time if your desire is more than just a vague ambition. If you are absolutely determined to become a *BAD A$$ CEO*, there's nothing that can stop you.

"BAD A$$ CEO" – EXERCISE APPENDIX-C

It's highly possible to take monumental steps toward high levels of prosperity, financial independence and inner peace with the money you are already bringing home. What could your children and your children's children accomplish if you set your family free from the bondage of debt? By answering the following questions truthfully, you can take your financial life to the next level and you and your family can be financially secure regardless of a fluctuating economy.

- Can you see how operating on 100 percent cash can benefit you more than using credit? (Save $1000 as fast as you can to use as an emergency fund to cover emergencies with cash without having to go into debt.)

- Are you willing to sell some stuff or work an extra job to do whatever it takes to focus your resources on debt elimination? (Track your spending on items such as food, groceries, insurance, clothes and recreation to determine where you can cut expenses to determine how much extra money could be applied towards debt elimination.)

- Think about all the money that is currently going out in the form of debt payments (credit cards, furniture, car loans, mortgage, etc.). How would it feel if you actually got to keep all that money every month? What could you do with it? (List all of your debts except your house then prioritize them to pay off the smallest balance through the largest balance.)

- Are you willing to sacrifice extra money to pay the absolute maximum amount that you can until the debt is gone? (Make the regular payment plus the extra money on the smallest balance until it is paid off while making the minimum payments on all of your other debts.)

- Are you willing to discipline yourself to repeat the process again and again until all of your debts have been eliminated? (When the first debt is paid off maintain focus by using the money from the debt you paid off to pay on to the next debt, then the next debt and so on.)

Most people aren't living their life's dreams because they have to pay bills. Imagine having absolutely no debt, no car payments, no credit card payments, or even a house payment. Your BAD A$$ CEO attitude gives you the power and the privilege to eliminate your debt and transform your life. Again, if you didn't have bills what would you do with all that money?

STEP FOUR

Stop believing that you are who society told you that you are supposed to be and create your own opportunity

BAD A$$ CEO!

"The question isn't who is going to let me; it's who is going to stop me!"

~Ayn Rand

Chapter Four

THE FEELING OF FLYING WITHOUT
THE FEAR OF FALLING

(Set your sights high and let the world know)

Everybody experiences not wanting to wait to be let into something, so deep inside you develop the attitude that you have to kick in the door and take what you want. That's what *BAD A$$ CEO* is all about. It's about not caring if you are accepted. It's about not giving a fuck. Just stepping up and doing what you need to do to take what is yours. Not in a scary, bad way, but in a positive entrepreneurial way! America offers dreams and nightmares, ease and struggle, trial and tribulation. The harsh reality is that if you want to have control over your life, over your destiny, the only way to do that is to have something of your own. Entrepreneurship surrounds us. New businesses and ventures are the very pulse of wealth around the world. I recognized this early on and I didn't want to just survive, I wanted to thrive. I wanted to have something of my own and I wanted to be judged by what I would be able to do by having something that I owned. When you have that dream, that fire, that need to change your current situation; it's hard to get rid of it. You have something to say to the world. You have a contribution to make. In my line of work, Information Entrepreneurs have emerged as the greatest wealth builders ever. They are making untold billions of dollars moving information instead of tangible goods. Entrepreneurship is the single biggest source of wealth in this country and *BAD A$$ CEO* is your blueprint to thriving. Using my concept of being a *BAD A$$ CEO* and thinking outside of the box you have an opportunity to establish yourself as a producer and owner of resources…transcending your own limits and never again believing in the impossible.

*BAD A$$ CEO*s see the world through the eyes of a business owner and an investor, not as a worker who works for a business. Regardless of your current situation, you are working with essentially, a blank page, which means you can experiment and fine-tune a style that is indicative of yourself. Your most important product is you so if you have a passionate belief about yourself it's motivating, it's persuasive, it's convincing and I think it's the best way to live. How many of you have given up your dreams in order to follow a more secure and socially accepted path? It's time to come out from behind the throne and wield the power that has your name on it.

MAKE A BUSINESS DECISION

If today always feels like yesterday and you can't see a new tomorrow, then guess what? You are what needs fixing. The point is; you have the power to transform your shit at the snap of a finger. Building a business as an asset is one of the most powerful forms of wealth generation and one of the best steps you can take to address your employment and wealth needs and create a thriving economy for yourself. The basis of wealth is the ownership and control of resources and there is no stopping someone that will stop at nothing; so if you want something you have to decide how to get it because no one else is going to get it for you. There is no stronger motivator for economic empowerment than the knowledge that, right now at this very moment *BAD A$$ CEO*s are out there in the world training, grinding, masterminding and employing every resource at their disposal, and weapon in their arsenal, to try to seize a strategically competitive position, by building jobs, products and services that satisfy consumers' basic needs and desires. I believe everyone has a message and a life story or experience that can help other people. You have a message too… your unique voice and contribution. Even if you haven't discovered it or defined it yet, you have something in you that you can deliver to the world. In terms of a *BAD AŞŞ CEO* career, being an Information Entrepreneur can be extremely lucrative because people will always need help and advice in their personal and professional lives. There is no limit to how many people will search for and need your knowledge and information.

In *BAD BOYS FINIŞH RICH* I showed you the five steps to creating a *BAD BOYS FINIŞH RICH* empire and screamed it at you, and in *REBELLIOUŞ WEALTH* I showed you how to package your strategies for success and how-to knowledge to create your own economy. So now, let me show you my single most important strategy for launching an information business and becoming a *BAD AŞŞ CEO*. Let's begin one of the most exciting ventures on your wealth building journey.

ANALYZING THE PLAYING FIELD
FOR LEVERAGE TO EXPLOIT

The theme and concepts of my books teach and show you what I did to become an Information Entrepreneur and create my own Information business, but my intent is not that you completely follow in my foot-steps. I simply want you to do what I did when I faced the pain of wanting to empower myself and create your own game within the game. Whether that means starting your own business or just being more self-reliant. Please don't confuse my extreme confidence with arrogance, but I am extremely confident that this material works because many people are benefiting from it. Please don't look for some big revelation or new principles. What I teach is truth and the principles I teach are changing lives. My aim is to carefully weave inspiration and information together into a step-by-step plan and this book is process driven.

I feel strongly that everyone should strive for some measure of financial freedom. It's natural to want to improve our circumstances and enjoy the best life has to offer. Unfortunately for many, the prison of not being able to do so is entirely self-imposed. The key is right between our ears. It sounds counterintuitive, but you need to recalibrate your thinking. If developed and leveraged this one thing has the potential to create unparalled success and prosperity in every dimension of life. Yet it is the least understood, most neglected and most underestimated. Its value can hardly be overstated.

As you know I am passionate about self-reliance. What topics have you studied and been fascinated by in your life? You probably have multiple areas that you can claim, but if you are going to be a *BAD A$$ CEO* you need to pick one topic, learn it, master it, share it, become known for it, and make real money teaching it. Choose one topic to be known for and develop your information business on that one topic. The easiest way to do this is to surf through social media and take note of what problems your friends are talking about. Take a piece of paper and draw a line down the middle. On one side, write down the most common problems. In the second column, make a similar list of what problem is causing them the most pain. Take a look at your list and see which problems you can solve quickly and turn that problem into your product. This will allow you to be your own job and product producer instead of always seeking the jobs and products of others. When you become production-oriented rather than consumption-oriented, you define the terms and you choose the work.

What have you been through in life? I share from personal experience. I want to find people similar to me, who are passionate about the same topics I am, want to learn the same things that I do, and who have been through similar struggles that I have; so I ask myself what audience would most likely benefit from training on a topic like mine and what audience would most likely pay for training on a topic like mine? My goal is to engage you further, both intellectually and soulfully, fostering your inner wisdom so that you can see things clearly and make better choices in your life. I want to provide a sense of direction for mobility, a tool to capture new financial territory and a mechanism to control an economic industry. I owe it to you to teach you things that will better your lives so I want to instill a mind-set that encourages you to concentrate and direct your resources for maximum, impact and benefit. That may give you a clue why I consider the book you are holding in your hands essential reading. Since you've picked it up, it's safe to assume you already know there's more to a genuine sense of wealth than just working, saving and investing. For many, this subject matter is deeper and more controversial than normal financial communications. Why? Because it takes us beyond the core competence of normal financial literacy with no expectation of the norm. This kind of wealth guidance is priceless because it titillates you with nuggets of truth and lessons that you can apply to your own life here and now. If your experience is typical, you won't just enjoy it, you'll tell your family and friends about it and give it as a gift.

MAKING SENSE OF THE VERY COMPLEX AND OFTEN CONFUSING QUEST FOR WEALTH

The only real way to learn how to run an Information business is by running an Information business and the only thing you don't have is the way, the right way to make a lot of money from what you already know. *BAD A$$ CEO* will help you do just that. Information will be the world's great wealth producer in the foreseeable future and you can create profits and wealth by simply creating specialized information. You can build special industries and become producers to eradicate your non competitiveness. There is no doubt that great opportunity for profit exists as an Information Entrepreneur and using out-of-the-box thinking, your products can produce power and wealth. Take heed to the words of Jazz musician Miles Davis, "When you're creating your own shit, man, even the sky ain't the limit." Armed with a new vision and tools, your intent should be to own and control and to control as much as possible. Ideally, you want to own and control every level of an industry through the application of your concept. Although it is beyond the scope of this book to develop detailed business plans, these suggestions serve as an example of the way *BAD A$$ CEO* principles can be used to transform weakness into power by getting others to play with your cards that you deal.

TELL ME AGAIN WHY I CAN'T
DO WHAT I AM ALREADY DOING

It's not always necessary to reinvent the wheel in order to start a successful Information business. I haven't invented anything new. What I have done is packaged what I have learned into a process that is doable and that inspires people to act on it. Most of us know what to do, we just have trouble doing it. Amazon's suite of services makes it possible for me, you and many other Information Entrepreneurs to bypass traditional publishing companies. It gives us the tools to create and sell digital books; print and sell paperback copies on demand; add author pages and even market books. So the sale of this book extricates me from mediocrity because this book is a business system that has unlimited leverage in both time and money. It survives time and it is capable of earning income long after my original investment of the time it took me to write it. This book effectively transfers the act of income generation from me the human asset to the book the business asset. So you can't stand still. If you do, life will pass you by. Don't wait for the right time or the perfect time. It will never happen. You have to constantly challenge yourself to achieve greater and greater accomplishments to become the owner and beneficiary of what your labor produces. I have bought and read many books on the subject of wealth building and self-reliance while I took action. Did the authors of those books tell me big ideas that were ground breaking? No, they simply gave me an action plan and some supporting details to what I already knew had to be done. A revolution is evolving and offers you a chance to improve your status so set your own direction in your own best interest. It bears repeating: The same skills that allow you to survive, if used pro-actively can enable you to thrive. Most people live on the other side of the coin. If you live the way I teach you in this book, you will prosper in good times and in bad times. You can take control of information to compete in a competitive society. You are in a position to commercialize your assets, to build wealth, income, employment and business opportunities. Life is a game; a game that I take seriously, but a game nonetheless; so be a *BAD A$$ CEO* and stand out beyond the masses.

"BAD A$$ CEO" – EXERCISE APPENDIX-D

Take an asset and build a system around it. Most people do not know how to set up a business like that. I say this to illustrate that this chapter has taught you how to do that. Every problem is a product. Find the problem and sell the solution. This same concept will work for you. The following questions will help you position yourself to develop an Information business and discover your own information product topics and ideas. After you have answered these questions take it one step further with self-reflection and research to gain clarity and figure out the best possible direction for you and then ambitiously pursue your own self-direction. Let the power of your *BAD A$$ CEO* attitude take you where you want to go, do what you want to do and create the lifestyle you want to live.

- The topics I have always studied and been fascinated by are…

- People on social media often dream of achieving…

- Something I have always wanted to learn more about is…

- People on social media are afraid of not knowing enough about…

- Things that I have been through in my life that might inspire people are…

- People on social media often pay good money for…

- The topic I would love to help people with is…

- The thing that seems to frustrate people on social media the most right now is…

- If I could give people I know information that would help them improve their lives, they would probably want strategies on how to…

- Based on my answers to the previous questions, how-to-information that I could provide to people I know that would help them would include strategies on how to…

STEP FIVE

Embrace who you are and always be the baddest mothefucker in the room

BAD A$$ CEO!

"When I get old and my grandchildren ask me what was Ray Bolden really like? With a smile on my face and all the love I can have for them, I'm going to say, I just want to let you guys know that Ray Bolden was a bad motherfucker!"

~ Ray Bolden

Chapter Five

DROP THE MIC

(Act like you own the whole fucking world)

In our competitive society, why would the power holders want to throw the doors of economic opportunity wide open to you? This is not the nature of competitors who play the game of I have mine and I am also going to take yours. We live in a world of winners and losers. A world of I'm smart and you're not. A world of I win, not we win. The world is a competitive place and there are few if any incentives for others to intentionally make decisions in your best interest. So you must do the next best thing: take advantage of the fact that you are outside the mainstream economy, and construct your own parallel alternative economy. Those people who do not understand how an economy is built and operates automatically surrender all of their wealth-building power to those who understand. So when you don't have power, it gnaws at you once you fully understand that you don't have it. So let us faithfully believe that our dreams are worth any struggle and that it is our time to free ourselves and rise to prominence. This journey that I have taken you on is one that gives you a perspective on what being a *BAD A$$ CEO* means, what it looks like and what is painfully obvious to achieve self-actualization, economic empowerment, and a true sense of freedom because without your own power, it is impossible for you to compete. If we can unchain ourselves from our own self-imposed restrictions, we can have that day and express our power.

There comes a time in the lives of those of us who are destined for greatness when we must stand in front of the mirror and ask: Why, do we live as mice, when we have been endowed with the courageous heart of a lion? We must look ourselves dead in the face and ask why we waste so much time paying attention to distractions that don't empower us economically, and why we think it's ok to play small when it comes to our money and our lifestyles. We must ask why we subordinate ourselves and allow ourselves to be mediocre when being a *BAD A$$ CEO* offers unlimited freedom, power and abundance to the bold, the determined, the creative and the independent. At first you may refuse to believe that this strange new thing can be done, and then you will begin to hope it can be done, then see it can be done. Then when it is done you will wonder why you didn't do it a long time ago. What I'm talking about is real. This is serious! You either get it or you don't. You've got to understand that it's less a physiological condition and more a framework for approaching your day-to-day life. You don't have time for anything except what's going to move you forward, but like any new habit or system, it requires practice, discipline and repetition to experience it's power firsthand. Once you start to understand *BAD A$$ CEO*, or even just recognize it, you will begin to see the world in a different way.

HOW TO BE THE BADDEST MOTHERFUCKER IN THE ROOM

✓ BAD A$$ CEOs have different values!
✓ BAD A$$ CEO's play their own games!
✓ BAD A$$ CEOs use their resources and talent!
✓ BAD A$$ CEOs fight for some form of liberation!
✓ BAD A$$ CEO's create their own system of order!
✓ BAD A$$ CEOs dare to be creative and spontaneous!
✓ BAD A$$ CEOs demand a return on their investment!
✓ BAD A$$ CEOs work for cash flow not capital gains!
✓ BAD A$$ CEOs believe they control their own destinies!
✓ BAD A$$ CEOs are dedicated to some form of freedom!
✓ BAD A$$ CEO's challenge what has been labeled normal!
✓ BAD A$$ CEOs remain true and strong despite temptation!

- ✓ BAD A$$ CEO's have a complete disdain for the status quo!
- ✓ BAD A$$ CEO's don't get stuck and don't acknowledge rules!
- ✓ BAD A$$ CEOs don't have jobs. BAD A$$ CEOs create jobs!
- ✓ BAD A$$ CEOs come up with multiple answers to solve problems!
- ✓ BAD A$$ CEOs know when to throw punches and when to roll with them!
- ✓ BAD A$$ CEOs train themselves to be free from social and self-oppression!
- ✓ BAD A$$ CEO'S place more value on what's in their bank accounts and stock portfolios than what is in their garage or closet!
- ✓ BAD A$$ CEOs are independent, unique and genuine as they serve the world!
- ✓ BAD A$$ CEOs refuse to recant their beliefs and quit the fight for independence!
- ✓ BAD A$$ CEOs know where they are going and do it while having fun along the way!
- ✓ BAD A$$ CEOs think seriously about how they create, conserve and invest their money!
- ✓ BAD A$$ CEOs strike a balance between financial literacy, discipline and money management!
- ✓ BAD A$$ CEOs use their minds to think for themselves and don't just go along with the program!
- ✓ BAD A$$ CEOs settle for no less than to seek and find their own economic and personal freedom!
- ✓ BAD A$$ CEOs figure out how to dramatically increase their fair market value through trial and error!
- ✓ BAD A$$ CEOs declare their rights, direction and independence without apologies. Their only guide is an internal one!

✓ BAD A$$ CEOs understand that they are the center of their own control. They don't need permission. They are their own self-appointed leader!

BAD A$$ CEO is a gift that isn't just a thing, but a prized possession; an artifact that becomes a part of your story, your narrative, and being a *BAD A$$ CEO* is the greatest dream ever voiced. It's a giant leap of mankind and is supplied to counteract what's offered by society. I'd rather be ruled by my own *BAD A$$ CEO* attitude than the other noise out there fighting to control my life. The greatest benefit of being a *BAD A$$ CEO* is that only you can judge yourself and I see my role as connecting you to being "Bad" and giving you the knowledge and help you need to know when to follow the rules and when to rewrite them. I want you to be able to use your *BAD A$$ CEO* attitude to project yourself into a life where you can do whatever you want because someone somewhere is always already doing it. The bigger question is; will you do it too?

FUCK YOU! THE WORDS THAT SET ME ON A PATH TO SUCCESS

I would love to tell you that my success was fueled completely by passion and creativity instead of aggression and ambition, but that would be a lie and this book is about uncensored honesty. It took me a long time to get to the top of my own food chain. I was ambitious and eager, but I was also sloppy and unorganized. The most amazing part of my journey though is that I turned the struggles of my own life into a series of books like this. I want you to understand what separates *BAD A$$ CEO*s from losers. You've been told for so long that the path to success was paved with a series of boxes that you have to check off, starting with getting a degree and getting a job and if you fail at these you are destined to lose in life. Don't get me wrong, I will be the first to admit that I have been fortunate in so many ways, but I must stress that none of this was an accident. I always knew that I was capable of something bigger, destined for something greater. That something turned out to be becoming a *BAD A$$ CEO*, but you know what? I didn't find *BAD A$$ CEO*, I created it. I'm telling my story to remind you that the straight and narrow is not the only path to success. I tried the obvious routes of college and the military, and sure it worked to a certain degree, but not at the level that I needed. What I thought I wanted and needed heading into that experience was totally different than what I actually required to reach the next level. I needed to somehow convey that I was different because only a lion is convinced of his invincibility. Everybody else walks through the jungle scared that, at any moment, a more powerful animal could jump out from behind a tree and eat them. This made me think bigger, I had something different in mind. It wasn't me who needed to slow down, it was everyone else who needed to keep up. My challenge was to shape the world to adapt to me, not the other way around. Although my methodology wasn't even close to being academically sound, I was the only guy around with a thesis on the subject and therefore the only expert. I learned to flip an obstacle into a benefit. This was me trying to define my own personal brand. Initially I wasn't thinking long term. There was no strategy, just hustle. This was me just figuring things out as I went along looking for a way to maximize my investment in myself because I love myself to much to accept anything less than the absolute best out of life and I want you to feel the same way. It's easy to feel sorry for ourselves and it's even easier to think about all the unfortunate things that happen to us and all the bad situations we find ourselves in. Sometimes we think that these situations are completely out of our hands and that we are simply victims of fate. But these are simply excuses we tell ourselves because we are afraid to accept that we can control our lives.

So that's how things happened for me, developing my own persona and working it to my advantage. No doubt some people will say that I am lucky: True, but I was just as insecure and scared as the rest of the world, and I am lucky in the sense that I had the courage to do what had to be done to get to where I am today. We are all meant to be wild independent and free. The day is meant to be ours and our purpose within it is to live as who we truly are and enjoy life's freedoms as we chase our meaning and purpose... our own legacy. Sometimes you break the rules, sometimes you follow them, but always on your own terms.

ONLY THE ANIMALS AT THE TOP OF THE FOOD CHAIN CONTROL THEIR DESTINY

Let me be brutally honest, your belief or disbelief in *BAD A$$ CEO* doesn't change my reality; it only changes yours. Ok, I won't get taken seriously by asking you to take me seriously so let me repeat that: What you think of being a *BAD A$$ CEO* doesn't change my reality; its purpose is to change yours because if you can't see the opportunities that surround you every day then you aren't using your *BAD A$$ CEO* attitude. Being a *BAD A$$ CEO* is more art than science, but you need to develop your own system. And that is the reality that you face. Always asking for permission, not making waves, denying your ambition, always doing what you are told and always following the rules can throw a roadblock into your path to power. Abandon anything about your life and habits that might be holding you back and learn to create your own opportunities, be who you want to be and do what you want to do. *BAD A$$ CEO* is presented with cynicism and while it's opinionated, it ultimately presents the truth. It might insult, offend or challenge you, but that's only because it violates everything you've that you've been taught. As an artist, this is what I like to paint. If you don't like my paintings, then they're not for you. They're not for everyone, but the whole purpose is to make sure I continue the path that I am on. When it's all said and done, my purpose is to offer you the information that will allow you to have all the things in life that you deserve. By understanding the principles we've discussed and then by incorporating them into your life, I'm convinced you will improve the quality of your life beyond your wildest dreams. My wish for you is that the principles in this book give you the knowledge, the wisdom and the understanding to recognize your own worth. Most of all, I wanted to share my spirit of being bad with you. In the words of hip hop pioneers RUN DMC, "Not bad meaning bad, but bad meaning good!" It's the core value of my company BOLD Ambition Worldwide. Allow me to say thank you for your support and trust in my brand. It's because of you and your support that we've grown the way that we have and are building a foundation on which my empire can continue to expand. I won't attempt to measure the success of this book by whether or not it becomes a bestseller, but by how many lives it touches. If it causes someone to have the courage to stand up, hold their heads high, stick their chest out, be bad, and create their own opportunity, it will have served its purpose. Why do we need *BAD A$$ CEO*s? Because we are less than perfect and we are always looking for somebody that can be an example to us of what we can do and who we can be. That's why being a *BAD A$$ CEO* is so important. The question I ask myself is, am I pursuing my dreams and not compromising my goals and my vision. I don't want to wake up and know that the things that I always wanted to do; I stopped myself from doing them based on fear. Can you look in the mirror and honestly say that you are living up to your fullest potential? It breaks my heart when I look around and see the vast potential that is being untapped and under-used. I know life can be rough and it can get tough out there. Sometimes it can get downright ugly. I have walked a path like yours or some version of it, but know that you are designed for greatness. Once you discover the full value of being a *BAD A$$ CEO* you will become more than you ever dreamed. You are going to take over the world and change it in the process. You are... a *BAD A$$ CEO*!

82

BE A PART OF THE THOUSANDS OF LIVES CHANGED WITH THE HELP OF THE BAD BOYS FINI$H RICH PRINCIPLES!

Here's How It Works:

1. Once you receive your book, create a video of you holding up the book and enthusiastically saying the following:

I'm (First & Last Name) from (City & State or City and Country)! "Bad Boys or Bad Girls" Finish Rich! (Based on your gender)
I Got My Copy, Get Yours!

2. Post the video on Youtube.com.

3. Email the link of your video to admin@badboysfinishrich.com. Once we receive your video link and verify it for clarity and authenticity, we will add it to our growing list of videos.

Please Note: Please follow the script provided above. We reserve the right to reject and refuse any videos deemed substandard or inappropriate.

Visit **BADBOYSFINISHRICH.COM/bebad** for Examples!

FOLLOW RAY ON SOCIAL MEDIA

PERSPECTIVES ON FINANCIAL LITERACY AND ENTREPRENEURIAL EDUCATION THAT OFTEN CONTRADICT CONVENTIONAL WISDOM

Follow Ray on Facebook:

www.facebook.com/boldambitionworldwide

Follow Ray on Twitter:

www.twitter.com/IamMrBolden

Follow Ray on Amazon:

www.amazon.com/Ray-Bolden/e/B00VXC3YN4/ref=ntt_dp_epwbk_0

Please Note: After enjoying Ray's work, please provide a customer review and give feedback on Amazon.com.

Visit **BADBOYSFINISHRICH.COM/about_ray**

BOLD AMBITION
WORLDWIDE